Answers
to my
Mormon
Friends

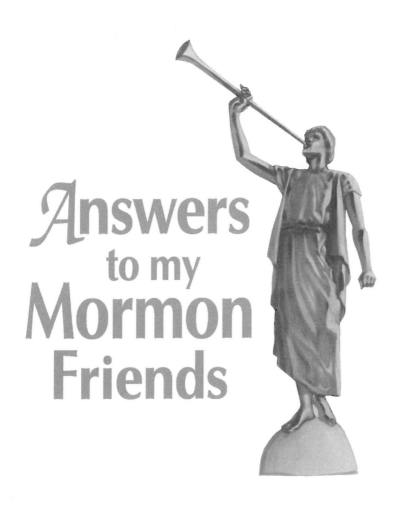

Answers
to my
Mormon
Friends

Thomas F. Heinze

CHICK
PUBLICATIONS

For a complete list of distributors nearest you
call us at (909) 987-0771 or visit us on the world
wide web at **www.chick.com**

© 2001 by Thomas F. Heinze

Published by:
CHICK PUBLICATIONS
P. O. Box 3500, Ontario, CA 91761-1019 USA
Tel: (909) 987-0771 • Fax: (909) 941-8128
www.chick.com
E Mail: postmaster@chick.com

Printed in the United States of America

ISBN: 0-758904-57-6

Seven Scriptures God wants you to know:

"...I am he: before me there was no God formed, neither shall there be after me." **Isaiah 43:10**

"For there is one God, and one mediator between God and men, the man Christ Jesus;" **1 Timothy 2:5**

"...Christ Jesus came into the world to save sinners..." **1 Timothy 1:15**

"For God so loved the world, that he gave his only begotten Son, that whosoever believeth in him should not perish, but have everlasting life." **John 3:16**

"Wherefore he is able also to save them to the uttermost that come unto God by him, seeing he ever liveth to make intercession for them." **Hebrews 7:25**

"For by grace are ye saved through faith; and that not of yourselves: it is the gift of God: Not of works, lest any man should boast. For we are his workmanship, created in Christ Jesus unto good works, which God hath before ordained that we should walk in them." **Ephesians 2:8-10**

"I do not frustrate the grace of God: for if righteousness come by the law, then Christ is dead in vain." **Galatians 2:21**

Contents

Chapter 3

Chapter 4

1

The Mormon Scriptures

Who Are The Mormons?

The Mormons are members of the Church of Jesus Christ of Latter-day Saints. They follow a religion founded by Joseph Smith, the first Mormon prophet, following a series of visions which started around 1820.

While they kept themselves separate during their early years, condemning all Christian churches and putting great emphasis on their prophet Joseph Smith, more recently there have been many changes in their culture and even a few changes in their doctrine.

Their emphasis now is much less on Joseph Smith and much more on Jesus Christ. As a Christian, I applaud and encourage this increased emphasis on Christ. I hope this direction will continue, and that many will come to trust Him completely and exclusively for their salvation.

In addition, where once Mormons were somewhat known for dysfunctional families with numerous downtrodden wives, in more recent years they have come to be admired for their strong emphasis on sound families and high moral values. In a world where alcohol and drug abuse abound, Mormons excel. A good Mormon does not even drink coffee or tea.

The Mormon's Scriptures

The Mormons have four books as their scriptures:
- The Bible, King James Version
- The Book of Mormon (My abbreviation: B of M)
- The Doctrine and Covenants
- The Pearl of Great Price.

The Mormons consider *The Book of Mormon* to be the most important of these books. In addition, the president of the Church is considered to be a living prophet.

Where Did The Book of Mormon Come From?

Joseph Smith said that an angel showed him *The Book of Mormon* written on gold plates in a language he called Reformed Egyptian.[1] He said that he translated these plates into English. The gold plates are not now available, and the Reformed Egyptian language is not known. The reason to believe that the plates once existed is faith in the word of Joseph Smith and eleven others who said they had seen them.

The Book of Mormon Introduction includes two statements. One, called "the testimony of the three

---

[1]*Book of Mormon*, Mormon 9:32. Also 1 Nephi 1:2, Mosiah 1:4.

witnesses" contains the names of the three. The second, called "the testimony of the eight witnesses" is followed by eight names. Both groups say they have seen the plates.

The first three witnesses, Oliver Cowdery, David Whitmer, and Martin Harris are given the most importance because *Doctrine and Covenants* predicted: "I will give them power that they may behold and view these things as they are; And to none else will I grant this power..." *The Book of Mormon* predicted:

> "...The book shall be hid from the eyes of the world that the eyes of none shall behold it save it be that the three witnesses shall behold it by the power of God... And there is none other which shall view it, save it be a few according to the will of God..."[1]

Doctrine and Covenants 17:2 says, "And it is by your faith that you shall obtain a view of them." By their faith, then, and by the power of God, the witnesses were to have viewed the plates.

Can we believe their witness? All of the three witnesses were excommunicated later by the Mormons themselves who accused them of lying, stealing, cheating, counterfeiting, defrauding, and persecuting the Mormons.[2]

---

[1] *Book of Mormon*, 2 Nephi 27:12-13
[2] *An Address to All Believers in Christ*, p. 27 as cited in Cowan, *Mormon Claims Answered*, 1997, p. 46, available from Utah Christian Publications, PO Box 71052, Salt Lake City, Utah 84171. See also Jerald and Sandra Tanner, *Mormonism, Shadow or Reality*, 1982, p. 52-53.

One of the Mormon's own scriptures, *Doctrine and Covenants*, has God saying that it was not wise to send Oliver Cowdery, the first of the three witnesses, carrying church money and a manuscript unless someone who was honest went with him (69:1). He later became a Methodist, and was eventually buried by a Methodist minister.

Another Mormon scripture went so far as to call Martin Harris, another of the three witnesses, a "wicked man" and a liar.[1] The Mormons themselves do not want to accept a later witness of David Whitmer:

> "In June 1838, God spoke to me again by His own voice from the heavens and told me to 'separate myself from among the Latter Day Saints.'"[2]

From time to time, Whitmer belonged to at least three Mormon splinter groups.

It seems clear that the three witnesses did say they saw the plates. The question is, can we believe their testimony? If we can believe the statements of Joseph Smith and other Mormon leaders about the character of these three witnesses, particularly the accusations that they were liars, there is little to give us faith in *The Book of Mormon* other than the word of Joseph Smith himself.

We will leave the three witnesses with Joseph Smith's blessing:

---

[1]*Doctrine and Covenants*, Introduction to Section 10, plus verses 1, 6-7, 13, 21.
[2]*An Address to All Believers in Christ*, p. 27, as cited by Marvin Cowan, *Mormon Claims Answered*, p. 46.

"Such characters as McLellin, John Whitmer, **David Whitmer, Oliver Cowdery**, and **Martin Harris** are too mean to mention; and we had liked to have forgotten them."[1]

David Whitmer, one of the first three witnesses, wrote that all of the second group of eight witnesses who were then living, except Joseph's father and two brothers, had left the Church of Latter-day Saints.[2]

Correcting the Most Correct Book

Protestants, Catholics, and Mormons all consider the Bible the inspired word of God. The original Hebrew and Greek documents of the Bible no longer exist, but there are many ancient copies. Great effort is made to compare these copies to one another to determine which copies reflect the original, and which contain errors in copying. The object is to determine what the original Old Testament Hebrew and the original New Testament Greek actually said.

The introduction to *The Book of Mormon* states that it was written by ancient prophets by the spirit of prophecy and revelation on gold plates. The plates were later, "delivered to Joseph Smith, who translated them by the gift and power of God." Smith is then quoted as saying,

"I told the brethren that *The Book of Mormon* was the most correct of any book on earth, and

---

[1]*History of the Church*, Vol. 3, p. 232.
[2]*An Address to All Believers in Christ*, p. 28, as cited by Marvin Cowan, *Mormon Claims Answered*, p. 47.

the keystone of our religion, and a man would
get nearer to God by abiding by its precepts,
than by any other book."

Though the English translation of *The Book of Mormon*
serves as the original from which other translations are
made, Mormon leaders have made over 4,000 corrections
in Smith's translation. Many of the changes were made to
correct embarrassing spelling and grammatical errors such
as "...Adam and Eve, which was our first parents."
Mormon Apostle B.H. Roberts wrote,

> "Are those flagrant errors in grammar
> chargeable to the Lord? To say so is to invite
> ridicule... That old theory cannot be
> successfully maintained; that is that the Urim
> and the Thummim did the translating, the
> prophet nothing beyond repeating what he saw
> reflected in that instrument."[1]

Other corrections were added as Joseph Smith's view of
God changed. For example, "mother of God" in the
original 1830 version becomes "mother of the Son of
God" (*B of M*, 1 Nephi 11:18). And "King Benjamin"
becomes "King Mosiah" (*B of M*, Ether 4:1).

Instead of trying to determine and maintain the original
just as Smith had first written it, as is the case with the
Bible, Mormon leaders felt that it needed correction. After
cleaning up the grammar, and correcting other mistakes,

---

[1]*Defense of the Faith*, pp. 278-279, 295,
306-308, as cited in Cowan, p. 41.

some Mormon leaders tell people that since Joseph Smith had little education, he would have to have had divine guidance to have written *The Book of Mormon* so well!

Jerald and Sandra Tanner's website, Utah Lighthouse Ministries (www.utlm.org) will direct you to great quantities of well documented information, including many of the changes, plus links to images of the pages of the original 1830 *Book of Mormon* so you can compare them yourself. (www.irr.org/mit/changingscrips.html)

The eighth article in the Mormon statement of faith is:

> "We believe the Bible to be the word of God as
> far as it is translated correctly; we also believe
> *The Book of Mormon* to be the word of God."

While Mormons tell outsiders that they believe the Bible, and it is in the list of the four books they accept as scripture, in practice, the Bible gets downgraded. When a point comes up in the conversation in which Mormon belief contradicts the Bible, Mormons are often taught that in that point, the Bible must have been translated incorrectly.

In practice the Bible is subordinated to *The Book of Mormon* and to today's Mormon teachings. Speaking of the Bible, *The Book of Mormon* states:

> "…after the book hath gone forth through the
> hands of the great and abominable church, that
> there are many plain and precious things taken
> away from the book, which is the book of the
> Lamb of God."[1]

---

[1] *Book of Mormon*, 1 Nephi 13:28.

The explanation is given that this means the Catholic Church changed the Bible so that many parts of it are no longer trustworthy.

It is easy to check out that idea. Many parts of the Hebrew Old Testament were found among the Dead Sea Scrolls which had been hidden at various times from 100 BC to 100 AD in caves near the Dead Sea. They remained there until 1946 when the first of these manuscripts was found. The scrolls of the Bible were among the oldest of the Dead Sea Scrolls. These parts of the Bible were hidden before there was a Catholic Church, and found relatively recently, so they could not have been changed. No "plain and precious things were taken away from" the Old Testament.

This leaves only the New Testament, and there are more ancient documents of the New Testament still in existence than of any other ancient book. How could any church have gathered up and changed all those copies? Mormons claim that specific changes which they mention were made in translating the Bible. No old Greek or Hebrew manuscript of the Bible of any age backs up these claims.

The only translation of the Bible that the Catholic Church accepted up through the time of the Protestant Reformation was the Latin Vulgate, translated by Saint Jerome around 400 AD. From that time until the last few hundred years, Catholics opposed any new translations of the Bible, so only Protestants translated it. Protestants translated directly from the Greek and Hebrew, not from anything the Catholic Church could have changed. Therefore, while the Catholic Church could have influenced the translation of the Latin Vulgate, and other translations which depended on the Vulgate, they could not change the Protestant translations which are the great majority.

I read from the Hebrew Old Testament and the Greek New Testament every day, not as an expert but as a student. Since these are the original languages of the Bible, I can say from personal experience that the differences between what Mormons believe and the Bible are not caused by mistranslations of the Bible.

The Bible has been translated into more languages than any other book. You can check different translations of the Bible in every language you know. They use different words to express the meaning of the original, but you will never find one translation that says "King Benjamin" where another translates "King Mosiah." though this change was made in *The Book of Mormon*. If one book should be considered inferior to the other because of translation problems, the Bible should be honored above *The Book of Mormon*, not the other way around.

Like *The Book of Mormon*, the other official Mormon Scriptures, *Doctrine and Covenants* and *The Pearl of Great Price* have also undergone many corrections. As I will point out later, in many instances where Mormon doctrine contradicts the Bible, it also contradicts *The Book of Mormon*, and sometimes the first part of *Doctrine and Covenants*. In these cases Mormon leaders tend to criticize the Bible, saying it was translated incorrectly, while ignoring the same contradictions with their other two books.

Mormons usually say they know that Mormon beliefs are correct because they have been taught to pray that the Holy Ghost would give them the testimony, that is, knowledge received by revelation from the Holy Ghost, which teaches them that the Church of Jesus Christ of Latter-day Saints is "the only true and living church upon the face of the whole earth."[1]

Some have prayed for the testimony, and feel that they have it and that Mormonism is right, but others who have prayed feel just as strongly that it is wrong. Still others think they have received the testimony that one or another of the Mormon splinter groups is the true church. God has told me, by His Spirit and through the Bible, that in the points where Mormon doctrine contradicts the Bible, Mormon doctrine is wrong.

Why should we pray for this testimony only about Mormonism and *The Book of Mormon*? How about Islam and the Koran? The Jehovah's Witnesses, Scientology? We need God's guidance, but people who rely on their feelings and purposely ignore the objective evidence can often be manipulated into believing things that are not true.

When Jesus Christ rose from the dead, he did not ask His disciples to believe in His resurrection only on the basis of the testimony of the Holy Ghost. He also showed them His hands and his feet, and ate in their presence. The evidence supported the testimony. If a testimony really is from the Holy Ghost, it is true, and the physical evidence will confirm, rather than refute that testimony.

It is easy to check out the evidence that confirms or refutes Smith's ability as a translator. Whether or not the

---

[1]*Doctrine and Covenants,* 1:30

gold plates of *The Book of Mormon* and its language "Reformed Egyptian" really existed, Smith later acquired a real ancient Egyptian manuscript. It was not written in hieroglyphics, but in the script called hieratic which came into use after hieroglyphics. Smith claimed to have translated this manuscript. He called the translation The Book of Abraham, written by the Abraham of the Old Testament. It is the second part of *The Pearl of Great Price*, one of the Mormon scriptures.

The manuscript, a papyrus, was thought to have been lost in the Chicago fire, but later found its way into the Metropolitan Museum of New York. Because it was identified by the Mormon Church as the one from which Smith had made his translation, the museum donated the papyrus to the Church.

The church's identification of the manuscript could hardly be in error because to protect the fragile papyrus, it had been backed in Smith's time with heavy old paper with writing on the back which helped the church to recognize it as authentic. This translation has given the church and the world the opportunity to put Smith's ability to translate Egyptian to the test.

A number of qualified Egyptologists have stated in writing that the manuscript made no mention at all of Abraham, but spoke instead of pagan funerals. One expert, Samuel A.B. Mercer, wrote:

> "All the scholars come to the same conclusion, viz. that Smith could not possibly translate any Egyptian text, as his translation of the facsimiles shows. Any pupil of mine who

would show such absolute ignorance of Egyptian as Smith does, could not possibly expect to get more than a zero in an examination in Egyptology..."[1]

Smith translated one word, which was the name of an Egyptian moon god, one hundred seventy seven different ways in different places in the text, none correctly.[2]

A Mormon named Grant Howard was excommunicated from the church for pointing out one letter which Smith had translated into seventy six words.[3]

Because these manuscripts show that neither Smith or any spirit that may have inspired him could translate Egyptian, some Mormons have denied that the manuscripts which were found were the same ones which Smith had "translated." This theory can quickly be eliminated two ways.

Smith included pictures from the manuscripts in three places in the Book of Abraham, a part of the Mormon scripture, *Pearl of Great Price*. (See pages 28, 34, and 42.) Smith wrote detailed explanations of the pictures which are there with them. Some of these pictures have writing on them, so Marvin Cowan sent them to experts who translated them and attested that they have nothing to do with Abraham, and that Smith's explanations are false.[4] You can send them to an expert too.

---

[1]Tanner, *Mormonism, Shadow or Reality?,* p. 321.

[2]Tanner, *Mormonism, Shadow or Reality?,* p. 323.

[3]Tanner, *Mormonism, Shadow or Reality?* p. 222-223.

[4]Marvin W. Cowan, *Mormon Claims Answered,* 1997, p. 53.

Also, photos were taken of the other pieces of papyri.[1] One includes the picture on page 28 of *Pearl of Great Price*, along with a good deal of writing on each side of the picture. It is undeniably the manuscript which Smith claimed to have translated. Since the engraved plates of *The Book of Mormon* are no longer with us, this is the only manuscript in existence by which we can judge whether or not Smith could translate Egyptian. He could not.

While Smith's statement about where his story of Abraham came from is not trustworthy, this does not mean that his whole book of Abraham is made up. Some of it comes from the King James Bible, which was translated into English from Greek and Hebrew in 1611. Compare Genesis 12:1-13 with Abraham 2 in *The Pearl of Great Price*. Smith made his "translation" some time after 1835 when he acquired the ancient Egyptian manuscript. If he had really translated this from Egyptian, how could he use old English expressions like "removed from thence?" This phrase is word for word the way it was translated in the King James Bible, first published two hundred years before Smith's "translation," and thousands of years after Smith said Abraham had written the book in Egyptian.

It should not be inferred that Smith copied the whole book of Abraham from the King James Bible. He did not. Some passages, however, like the two samples below are too close to King James English to be accidental:

> "Now the LORD had said unto Abram, Get thee out of thy country, and from thy kindred,

---

[1]You can see them in *Mormonism, Shadow or Reality?*, p. 295-297.

and from thy father's house, unto a land that I
will shew thee:" (Genesis 12:1).

Compare this to Smith's translation from *The Pearl of
Great Price*:

"Now the Lord had said unto me: Abraham, get
thee out of thy country, and from thy kindred,
and from thy father's house, unto a land that I
will show thee." (Abraham 2:3)

In this verse, only two words of Smith's "translation"
are different than the words of the King James Bible.
Compare also the first half of Genesis 1:30:

"And to every beast of the earth, and to every
fowl of the air, and to every thing that creepeth
upon the earth..."

The first half of Abraham 4:30 is identical.

"And to every beast of the earth, and to every
fowl of the air, and to every thing that creepeth
upon the earth..."

(Compare also Genesis 12:2 with Abraham 2:9; Genesis
12:3 with Abraham 2:11, Genesis 12:4 with Abraham 2:14.)

Smith must have copied these and other passages from
the King James Bible.

The Book of Abraham is important because:

• It shows that Joseph Smith was either
untruthful or seriously deluded in attributing
the source of the Book of Abraham to a
papyrus which had nothing to do with the
content of his Book of Abraham.

• It exposes Smith's inability to translate Egyptian, a very important fact, because Reformed Egyptian is the language from which he claimed to have translated *The Book of Mormon.*[1]

• The Book of Abraham is a source of the doctrine that blacks could not be allowed into the Mormon priesthood. While this doctrine has always been morally wrong, it later became politically incorrect, and an embarrassment to the Mormon church. L.D.S. President Kimball had a revelation in 1978 which reversed the doctrine.

The Book of Moses, another of the books in *The Pearl of Great Price*, has at least one whole page which is almost word for word the old English of the King James Bible. (Compare Moses 4:8-25 to Genesis 3:2-19.)

The prize for the longest section copied from the King James Bible, however, goes to 2 Nephi in *The Book of Mormon*. Chapters 12-24 are copied nearly word for word from Isaiah chapters 2-14, in all, about fifteen pages. The King James is an almost word for word translation from the Hebrew Old Testament and the Greek New Testament. In some places this does not make good English so the translators had to add some connecting words. To help us recognize what was in the original and what was not, the words they added were italicized in some editions, and put

---

[1]*Book of Mormon*, Mormon 9:32. Also 1 Nephi 1:2, Mosiah 1:4.

in brackets in others. Even these words which were not in the original Hebrew, but existed only in the King James Bible, ended up in *The Book of Mormon*.

Mormons are told: "Moroni deposited the plates in the Hill Cumorah in about 421 A.D"[1] If these plates were really hidden away over a thousand years before the King James Bible was translated into English, and Joseph had translated *The Book of Mormon* from those plates, how could he have translated hundreds of words, one after another, in exact King James English? Had he memorized that much of the Bible, or did he copy them?

History, Archeology, and The Book of Mormon

The Book of Mormon tells of groups of Jews who left the land of Israel and moved to what was probably Central America:

• The Jaredites left at the time of the Tower of Babel, and were eventually destroyed by wars.

• A group from the half tribe of Manasseh and from the tribe of Ephraim led by Lehi arrived around 589 B.C. They eventually split into two groups, the Nephites who were destroyed by war, and the Lamanites who became the ancestors of the Native Americans. (See the first two paragraphs of the Introduction to *The Book of Mormon*.)

The Book of Mormon is presented as true history and gives a number of details which we can check out. Mormons often claim that archeological discoveries

---

[1]McConkie, *Mormon Doctrine*, p. 327.

confirm the statements of *The Book of Mormon*. Many cities, mentioned in the Bible have indeed been uncovered by archeologists just where the Bible said.

However, no archeological evidence has been found in the Americas that directly verifies *The Book of Mormon*. Artifacts that have been found which could have been produced and used by the people of *The Book of Mormon*, could also have been produced and used by other people. Mormons have claimed, for example, that the Smithsonian Institution officially recognized *The Book of Mormon*, and that it had been used as the guide to almost all of the major discoveries. This generated so many inquires that the Smithsonian had to write out a stock answer which denies the claim. Here are a few excerpts:

> "...The Smithsonian Institution has never used *The Book of Mormon* in any way as a scientific guide. Smithsonian archeologists see no connection between the archeology of the New World and the subject matter of the book... We know of no authentic cases of ancient Egyptian or Hebrew writing having been found in the New World."[1]

As of 2001, the answer had been abbreviated to:

> "Your inquiry of February 7 concerning the Smithsonian Institution's alleged use of *The Book of Mormon* as a scientific guide has been received in this office for response. *The Book of*

---

[1] Tanner, *Mormonism, Shadow or Reality?*, p. 97-98.

Mormon is a religious document and not a scientific guide. The Smithsonian Institution has never used it in archeological research, and any information that you have received to the contrary is incorrect. Your interest in the Smithsonian Institution is appreciated."

The Languages

According to *The Book of Mormon*, the languages spoken by the first people to live in the Americas were Hebrew and Egyptian. If this were true, at least some of the native American languages should contain words which clearly show this origin. English has thousands of words which contain Greek and Latin roots. After two thousand years these roots still show the influences of Greek and Latin. If *The Book of Mormon* is correct, many Indian words should contain Hebrew and Egyptian roots. Many English words come to us from Spanish, French and the Germanic languages. Hebrew and Egyptian words, however, are not found in any of the Indian languages.

We use the Japanese word "tsunami" for tidal waves. Many such foreign words tend to creep into languages when there is some contact between the people, but Hebrew or Egyptian words did not creep into the native American languages.

The Hebrew immigrants, according to *The Book of Mormon*, knew how to read and write. If these really were the original languages it would seem probable that with all the archeological finds in Central America, manuscripts or inscriptions in Hebrew or Egyptian would be found. While

Mormons point to a few artifacts which may well have arrived from across the ocean, particularly from Japan, these artifacts do not indicate that the inhabitants of the Americas came from there.

I grew up near the Oregon coast, and remember that as a child it was a popular pastime to walk the beaches looking for blown glass fishing net floats which escaped from the nets and floated to our coast from the seas around Japan. The glass balls were rare enough to make them desirable, but most people who kept looking found a few. Much more would have been needed to validate any theory that the first inhabitants of Oregon came from Japan, just as much more than a few artifacts and a doubtful inscription are needed to show that the American Indians came from Israel.

The Animals

> "And it came to pass that we did find upon the land of promise as we journeyed into the wilderness that there were beasts in the forest of every kind, both the cow and the ox, and the ass and the horse, and the goat and the wild goat..."[1]

All the animals mentioned were imported to the Americas by Europeans after Columbus discovered America. None are believed to have lived in Latin America a few hundred years before and after the time of Christ when the

---

[1] *Book of Mormon*, 1 Nephi 18:25.

migrations of *The Book of Mormon* were to have taken place. Native animals, such as the Alpaca and the Llama, are never mentioned in *The Book of Mormon*.

The People

Many of the old inhabitants of the Americas are well known, the Incas, Aztecs, and the Mayas for example. None of these are mentioned in *The Book of Mormon*. It speaks instead of Jaredites, Nephites, and Lamanites. All are supposed to have come from the general area of Israel. None of these are mentioned in any other history of the new world. The Indians of America are, for the most part, of Mongolian origin.

In addition to the metals that people of the Americas are known to have used, *The Book of Mormon* says they also used iron and steel, implying an iron industry much larger than could be based on an occasional iron meteorite.[1] No iron industry in America in this period has been reported in history or found by archeologists. While it is possible that American Indians had iron and steel industries which left no trace, the fact that none have been found is an additional evidence to consider.

---

[1] *Book of Mormon*, Jarom 8; 2 Nephi 5:15.

2

Mormon Salvation

Smith's successor, Brigham Young once said, "There is the New Testament; you may leave out *The Book of Mormon* and the *Book of Doctrine and Covenants*, and follow the precepts of that book faithfully, and I will warrant you to arrive at salvation.[1]

He is right. Follow the Bible, and you will find salvation. The salvation of your soul is important, and the Bible is the word of God and is an accurate document. Remember:

• All the other books that Mormons recognize as Scripture have been revised through the years.

• *The Book of Mormon* contradicts the *Doctrine and Covenants*.

---

[1] *Journal of Discourses*, Vol. 1, p. 244, cited in *Mormon Claims Answered*, p. 32.

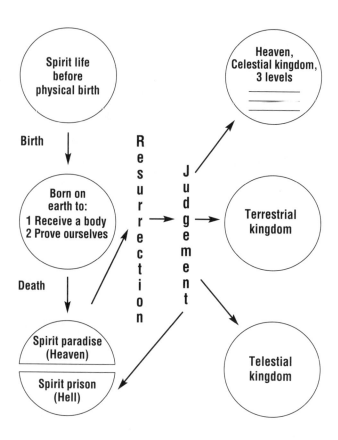

This diagram gives an overall idea of the Mormon world view, including their view of salvation. Follow the arrows from "Spirit life before physical birth," at the top left, all the way through the levels of salvation.

• The Egyptian manuscript from which Smith claimed to have translated the Book of Abraham was not written by Abraham, or about him, but tells about Egyptian funeral ceremonies. It shows that Smith could not translate Egyptian.

Salvation in the Mormon system depends on a complex mixture of grace, good works, baptism, other temple ceremonies, etc. which are not well understood even by most Mormons. Their theologians, however, have figured it out, and present a bit of it here, and a bit there.

To give you a handle on what Mormon doctrine teaches about salvation, I have relied heavily on the 856 page book, *Mormon Doctrine*, 1966 edition by Mormon apostle and theologian Bruce R. McConkie. To permit you to check up on me, but keep the references short, I have abbreviated the author and title to MMD, and followed it with the page number; for example: (MMD, p. 670). In the process of studying Mormon salvation, we will compare it on occasion to salvation in Christ as explained in the Bible.

Mormon doctrine teaches that at death a person goes into either spirit prison or spirit paradise. In prison he gets a second chance to accept the gospel. If he does, he can move up to spirit paradise. At the judgment he will be judged according to what he did in the flesh and assigned to one of a number of different levels: heaven, hell, etc. I have organized these levels in a descending order, starting with the highest heaven. I have summarized the Mormon belief about each level, and how to get there.

Celestial Glory

Mormons believe in "eternal progression," that is, that men are becoming gods, and that God Himself was once a man who became our God. McConkie quotes Joseph Smith:

> "God himself was once as we are now, and is an exalted man… God himself, the Father of us all, dwelt on an earth…"[1]

Within the celestial kingdom there are three distinct glories. Entrance into the lower level of the celestial kingdom requires faith, repentance, baptism, and receiving the Holy Ghost. (This level also includes children who die before the age of eight.)

To enter the middle level requires these same prerequisites, plus two ordinances which are performed in the Temple:

• "Initiatory," an ordinance of washing and anointing.

• "Endowments," special blessings, instruction and a holy garment received in a Mormon temple. These are administered not only for the living, but by proxy also for the dead.

The highest level of all is celestial glory, also called exaltation and eternal life. A person at this level has become a god, and gives birth to spirit children with which they will populate other worlds. "With few exceptions this is the salvation of which the scriptures speak."[2] For those who have all the prerequisites already mentioned, "Celestial Marriage is the gate to an exaltation in the

---

[1]MMD, p. 321.   [2]MMD, p. 670.

highest heaven within the celestial world."[1] This refers to being married in a Mormon temple. Other things McConkie mentions which one must have to enter are: Grace, obedience, good works, righteousness, devotion, sanctification, and faithfulness to the end."[2]

McConkie's idea of the salvation Christ offers by grace is vastly different than that of the Bible. He writes: "Immortality comes by grace alone, but those who gain it may find themselves damned in eternity." McConkie refers us to Alma 11:37-45, and continues: "Eternal life, the kind of life enjoyed by eternal beings in the celestial kingdom, comes by grace plus obedience."[3]

Terrestrial Glory

This second level of glory is no more than a reflection of the celestial glory. Those who are saved to this level remain unmarried and without exaltation eternally.[4] Those who go there must have lived an upright, honorable life, but fall into one of these categories:

• Those who die without law, and do not accept the gospel after physical death.

• Those who reject the gospel in this life but accept it in the spirit world.

• Honorable people who do not accept and live the gospel because they were blinded by the craftiness of men.

[1]MMD, p. 118
[2]MMD, p. 669-670
[3]MMD, p. 671
[4]MMD, p. 784

• Mormons who are not valiant in their devotion to the Church and to righteousness.

Telestial Glory

Most people end up in the tclestial kingdom, the lowest level of glory. These are the people who have not received the gospel.[1] In the Mormon system, Jesus Christ saves everybody, but from physical death only. That is, everyone will be resurrected and will be able to live somewhere after death. Where depends on the person's own works.

> "Those who gain only this general or un-conditional salvation will still be judged according to their works and receive their places in a terrestrial or a telestial kingdom. They will, therefore, be damned..."[2]

Only those who receive exaltation to the highest level of celestial glory and become gods receive full salvation.[3]

According to Mormon doctrine, who will be found in this lowest level of glory, which is also called damnation?

• Most adults who have ever lived: The proud, liars, thieves, sorcerers, adulterers, blasphemers and murderers.

• "After their resurrection, the great majority of those who have suffered in hell will pass into the telestial kingdom."[4]

---

[1]*Doctrine and Covenants* 76:101.
[2]MMD, p. 669.
[3]MMD, p. 670, *Book of Mormon*, Alma 11:37-41.
[4]MMD, p. 350.

Hell

The Prophet said, "The sectarian world are going to hell by hundreds, by thousands and by millions."[1]

"Among them are the sorcerers, adulterers, whoremongers, false swearers, 'those that oppress the hireling in his wages,' the proud, 'and all that do wickedly.'"[2]

"If they will not repent and believe in his name, and be baptized in his name, and endure to the end, they must be damned..."[3]

"Believers in the doctrines of modern Christendom will reap damnation to their souls..."[4]

"If it had not been for Joseph Smith and the restoration there would be no salvation. There is no salvation outside The Church of Jesus Christ of Latter-day Saints."[5]

Hell, according to Mormon doctrine, will have a much smaller population after the resurrection:

"After their resurrection, the great majority of those who have suffered in hell will pass into the telestial kingdom; the balance, cursed as sons of perdition, will be consigned to partake of endless woe with the devil and his angels."[6]

---

[1]MMD, p. 350-351   [2]MMD, p. 350.
[3]MMD, p. 177, quoting *Book of Mormon*, 2 Nephi 9:24
[4]MMD, p. 177   [5]MMD, p. 670   [6]MMD, p. 350

There is some difference of interpretation on this last point. Apostle John Widtsoe said:

"In the Church of Jesus Christ of Latter-day Saints, there is no hell. All will find a measure of salvation."[1]

Most Mormons would not go that far because *The Book of Mormon* says quite clearly that there is no deliverance from hell. It says that the devil whispers "there is no hell," while he deceives people and

"grasps them with his awful chains from whence there is no deliverance. Yea, they are grasped with death and hell...from whence they must go into the place prepared for them, even a lake of fire and brimstone, which is endless torment."[2]

The Book of Mormon and the Bible agree that hell is everlasting punishment from which none can escape. Fear of hell has led many to repent and turn to Christ for salvation, while others of all denominations try to convince themselves that Scripture is wrong and there is no hell.

Some Mormons have come up with the argument that hell is God's punishment, and God is eternal, and that this is the only sense in which hell is eternal punishment. Most would agree with McConkie that a relatively small

---

[1]*Evidences and Reconciliations*, 1960 edition, p. 216, as cited in Marvin Cowan, *Mormon Claims Answered*, p. 117.
[2]*Book of Mormon*, 2 Nephi 28:21-23. See also Alma 34:35.

number of sons of perdition will at the judgment be sent back to hell.

Reflecting on Salvation

As we reflect on salvation, dear Mormon friend, it is of the greatest importance that you know where you are going. The Mormon teaching about salvation is very complex and may discourage you from thinking this through, but the questions I want to ask you are vital to your future. Are you saved? Can you know that you have really done everything necessary for your salvation and will continue to do it faithfully until the end?

No system, Mormon or otherwise, can offer you the assurance of your salvation when the salvation it offers depends to a large degree on your efforts to save yourself. Why not?

> "All have sinned and come short of the glory of God" (Romans 3:23).

> "As it is written, There is none righteous, no, not one" (Romans 3:10).

You too have sinned. Perhaps you have sinned more than others, and perhaps less, but you have done some things that God sees as wrong, and may do more in the future, so you can't possibly know for sure that God will not judge you guilty.

The teachings of the Mormon Church make the hope of anyone's works being good enough even less certain:

> "It is very evident that church membership

alone will not keep an individual from one degree of damnation or another." This paragraph ends stating that he who doubts, or keeps a commandment with slothfulness, "the same is damned."[1]

Even the proud, the liars, and those who do not help the poor go to hell.[2] President Joseph F. Smith said he believes birth control is "one of the greatest crimes in the world today."[3] Since in Mormon doctrine your salvation depends in great part on your works, what chance do you have?

The good news is that Christ took upon Himself the judgment and punishment for your sin and mine. It is absolutely true that, "the wages of sin is death," but the really wonderful truth is, "but the gift of God is eternal life through Jesus Christ our Lord" (Romans 6:23). The gift becomes ours when we receive it by faith.

The salvation that God offers to sinners does not depend on our own power to keep God's law. "Therefore we conclude that a man is justified by faith without the deeds of the law" (Romans 3:28). Salvation is a gift that God gives to sinners who accept Christ by faith.

I may have confused you, but here is a passage that clears up the relationship between our faith in Christ and our works:

"For by grace are ye saved through faith; and that not of yourselves: it is the gift of God: Not

---

[1]MMD, p. 177, *Doctrine and Covenants* 58:26-29.
[2]MMD, p. 350.
[3]MMD, p. 86.

of works, lest any man should boast. For we are his workmanship, created in Christ Jesus unto good works, which God hath before ordained that we should walk in them" (Ephesians 2:8-10).

If our salvation depended on our putting aside a million dollars before we died, try as we might, most of us would never be able to do it, but if someone gave us the million dollars we would certainly be able to receive it.

We are not able to save our souls by only doing good works. God's laws make us see this. They shine a spotlight on our sins and help us to repent, believe, and receive the complete salvation that God, by His grace, offers us in Christ. It is a gift which we accept through faith.

When we accept that gift, our spiritual life starts, and Christ's Spirit molds our lives. The good works that we do result from the salvation which we have received as a gift. When we receive salvation, we become Christ's workmanship, and He guides our lives. He does not guide us to sin, but to do good works. This little train illustration makes it more clear.

Our salvation is not pulled in by our works, but our works are brought along by our salvation. (Ephesians 2:8-10)

The Bible says, "We conclude that a man is justified by faith without the deeds of the law" (Romans. 3:28). Don't count on your works being judged good enough. If you are a sinner, count on Christ who saves sinners. "Christ Jesus came into the world to save sinners" (1 Timothy 1:15). If you are trusting in your good life to save you, Christ is not the one that you are trusting to save you.

Neither is His salvation a halfway measure that leaves us damned. It does not just get us resurrected and then depend on our own works to get us saved.

> "Wherefore he is able also to save them to the uttermost that come unto God by him, seeing he ever liveth to make intercession for them" (Hebrews 7:25).

You will remember the thief on the cross that repented. He turned to Jesus and said: "Lord, remember me when thou comest into thy kingdom." Jesus did not say he would check the record to see whether the man had done enough good works. This man was being executed because he was a criminal. He turned to Christ because he knew that the kind of works he had done could never save anybody! He had not been baptized either.

Jesus told the thief on the cross who turned to Him, "Today shalt thou be with me in paradise" (Luke 23:43). That is what Jesus Christ really said to him. The passage has not been incorrectly translated as some Mormons have claimed. The original Greek word for paradise used here, spelled out in English letters, is "paradeiso." The English word "paradise" comes from it. You can check for yourself in a Greek/English New Testament. Jesus saved this sinner who turned to Him.

Once you are saved, God will help you do good works because you have been saved by grace through faith in the Savior, but your salvation does not depend on your works. It depends on Christ's ability to save. Let me illustrate this with another kind of salvation.

You are drowning in the ocean and call out to a lifeguard. He is jumping in to save you. Whether or not he will succeed will not depend on how good a person you have been. It will depend on the life guard's ability to swim. Shift your faith from your works to Jesus Christ. Accept Him as your Savior.

Does The Book of Mormon Speak of Temple Marriage?

This is one of the most important of Mormon doctrines. Without temple marriage a Mormon can not be fully saved. McConkie states:

> "Salvation in its true and full meaning is synonymous with exaltation or eternal life, and consists in gaining an inheritance in the highest of the three heavens within the Celestial Kingdom. With few exceptions this is the salvation of which the scriptures speak... This full salvation is obtained in and through the continuation of the family unit in eternity, and those who obtain it are Gods."[1]

---

[1]MMD, p. 670.

As gods, they are to give birth to spirit children with which they will populate other worlds. Because temple marriage is the key to Mormon salvation, McConkie emphasizes its importance:

> "The most important things that any member of the Church of Jesus Christ of Latter-day Saints ever does in this world are: 1) To marry the right person, in the right place, by the right authority; and 2) To keep the covenant made in connection with this holy and perfect order of matrimony– thus assuring the obedient persons of an inheritance of exaltation in the celestial kingdom."[1]

What McConkie means by this is that full salvation depends first of all upon marrying the right person in the Mormon Temple ceremony.

Mormon scripture says that *The Book of Mormon* contains the "fulness of the gospel,"[2] "the fulness of my everlasting gospel,"[3] and that almost all the doctrines of the Gospel are taught in it. But where in *The Book of Mormon* do you find that being married in the temple for time and eternity is the only way to have full salvation? The idea is not even mentioned!

In stark contrast to today's Mormon doctrine, many passages in *The Book of Mormon*, as in the Bible, teach that complete salvation is by faith in Jesus Christ, no temple marriage involved:

---

[1] MMD, p. 118.
[2] *Doctrine and Covenants* 20:9.
[3] *Doctrine and Covenants* 27:5.

"...remember that there is no other way nor means whereby man may be saved, only through the atoning blood of Jesus Christ, who shall come; yea, remember that he cometh to redeem the world."[1]

"And lo, he cometh unto his own, that salvation might come unto the children of men even through faith on his name."[2]

"And moreover, I say unto you that there shall be no other name given nor any other way or means whereby salvation can come unto the children of men, only in and through the name of Christ, the Lord Omnipotent."[3]

"...but men drink damnation to their own souls except they humble themselves and become as little children, and believe that salvation was, and is, and is to come, in and through the atoning blood of Christ, the Lord Omnipotent."[4]

These last two passages state not only that nothing else adds to a person's salvation, but that nothing ever will. This excludes the possibility that later revelation could substitute temple marriage as the way to complete salvation.

---

[1]*Book of Mormon*, Helaman 5:9.
[2]*Book of Mormon*, Mosiah 3:9.
[3]*Book of Mormon*, Mosiah 3:17.
[4]*Book of Mormon*, Mosiah 3:18. Follow the references from these passages to other similar passages.

The point that I want to make here is that *The Book of Mormon* never teaches about a temple marriage ceremony or that it has anything at all to do with our salvation, yet it is the book that is called, "the fulness of my everlasting gospel."[1]

The Book of Mormon is not alone. The Bible never mentions a temple marriage ceremony either. If temple marriage were really necessary for full salvation, and is the most important thing a Mormon does in this life, it would mean that both *The Book of Mormon* and the Bible completely missed the most important part of the gospel. They teach faith in Christ, not only for resurrection, but as the exclusive means of complete salvation.

Joseph Smith is introducing a different gospel: Full salvation depends on temple marriage. The Bible says:

> "But though we or an angel from heaven, preach any other gospel unto you than that which we have preached unto you, let him be accursed" (Galatians 1:8-9).

Are we saved by Christ, or marriage? The plot thickens!

How Many Wives?

After Smith had already finished *The Book of Mormon*, and almost all of *Doctrine and Covenants*, he was struck by the idea of having more than one wife, and wrote new scripture, Doctrine and Covenants 132, which commands that men marry more than one wife.

---

[1]*Doctrine and Covenants* 27:5. See also 20:9.

The first verse introduces the subject: "…I the Lord justified my servants Abraham, Isaac… as touching the principle and doctrine of their having many wives and concubines." He then says "…prepare thy heart to receive and obey the instructions which I am about to give unto you…"[1]

Having prepared the reader that these instructions were to be about having extra wives, the atomic bomb goes off in 132:4! I emphasize important points with bold print.

> "For behold, I reveal unto you a **new** and **everlasting** covenant; and if ye abide not in that covenant, then are ye damned; for **no one can reject this covenant and be permitted to enter into my glory**."

According to this passage of Mormon scripture, for all time, anyone who rejects the new covenant of plural wives cannot enter glory. Marriage to only one wife brings damnation.[2]

I have heard it argued that this is not really a new covenant, but just a detail added on to the covenants that had already been introduced. Smith did not say that. He called it "a **new** and **everlasting** covenant."

Joseph did not expect his wife Emma to be very enthusiastic about sharing him with other women, even though he was presenting it as a commandment which we are to keep or be damned. We see this in the way he keeps coming back to the subject all through this section, adding

---

[1]*Doctrines and Covenants* 132:3.
[2]*Doctrine and Covenants* 132:1-7, 32-34, 39-41.

one thing and another to convince her and the rest of us that God really commands men to have more than one wife.

In doing this, he ends up contradicting a very clear statement which he had written earlier in *The Book of Mormon*. There he had taught that polygamy, that is having more than one wife at the same time, is wrong, and is an abomination to God:

> "Behold, David and Solomon truly **had many wives and concubines, which thing was abominable** before me, saith the Lord. Wherefore, thus saith the Lord, I have led this people forth out of the land of Jerusalem, by the power of mine arm, that I might raise up unto me a righteous branch from the fruit of the loins of Joseph. Wherefore, I the Lord God will not suffer that the people shall do like unto them of old. Wherefore, my brethren, hear me, and hearken to the word of the Lord: **For there shall not any man among you have save it be one wife; and concubines he shall have none.**"[1]

Notice how clearly 132:39 contradicts this:

> "**David's wives and concubines were given unto him of me**, by the hand of Nathan, my servant, and others of the prophets who had the keys of this power; and **in none of these things did he sin against me** save in the case of Uriah and his wife..."

---

[1]*Book of Mormon*, Jacob 2:24-27.

The Book of Mormon clearly states that David's plural wives were an abomination before God. In direct contradiction, *Doctrine and Covenants* says that God gave him those wives and it was okay.

Arriving at 132:52 Smith has God say,

> "And let mine handmaid, Emma Smith, receive all those that have been given unto my servant Joseph…"

Smith has been building up to a climax, preparing people for the heart of his new teaching which is laid out in verses 61 and 62:

> "…If any man espouse a virgin, and desire to espouse another, and the first give her consent, and if he espouse the second, and they are virgins, and have vowed to no other man, then is he justified; he cannot commit adultery for they are given unto him… And if he have ten virgins given to him by this law, he cannot commit adultery, for they belong to him…"

Smith closes this section of Mormon scripture, (*Doctrine and Covenants* 132) with some threats of destruction against wives who don't want to accept the new everlasting covenant and share their husbands with other women. Emma seems to have given in as the *Encyclopedia Britannica* says of Joseph Smith,

> "…there is evidence that he may have married as many as 50 wives."[1]

---

[1]*Encyclopedia Britannica*, CD 98, from article "Joseph Smith."

The new and everlasting covenant of plural wives that everyone must accept or be damned was written in 1843. Because polygamy is illegal in the United States, the everlasting covenant lasted only until the United States government severely threatened the Church of Jesus Christ of Latter-day Saints if they did not stop the practice. The church backed down on October 6, 1890, when Wilford Woodruff, the president of the church said:

> "...I now publicly declare that my advice to the Latter-day Saints is to refrain from contracting any marriage forbidden by the law of the land."[1]

Will any Mormons who do not have more than one wife get into Glory? There are two possibilities:

• The covenant was called an "everlasting covenant" in Mormon scripture, but was only in effect for forty seven years, until a later Church president without exactly abrogating it, advised Mormons not to marry extra wives any more. Perhaps the new covenant is no longer in effect.

• The other possibility is that it is still in effect and only polygamists will receive full salvation. All other Mormons will be damned as 132:4 and 6 so forcefully insist.

It has been argued that the new covenant is not about plural wives, but I would remind them that right after the new covenant was given, both Smith, and most Mormon leaders, married extra wives, indicating that this was the normal interpretation of the passage. Who was better able

---

[1]This is found at the end of the book *Doctrine and Covenants*.

to understand the new covenant, Joseph Smith and the other Mormon leaders at the time, or people now who invent new meanings for the new covenant?

Most Mormons now comply with the law of the land and have just one wife on earth. Heaven is different. Mormon men may still marry a number of women for eternity in the temple. In that case, they are to be his wives and have many children when they all get to heaven.

In this point Mormon teaching is contrary to that of the Bible, which states:

> "Jesus answered and said unto them, Ye do err, not knowing the scriptures, nor the power of God. For in the resurrection they neither marry, nor are given in marriage, but are as the angels of God in heaven" (Matthew 22:29-30).

Mormons can hardly blame their difference with the Bible in this point on a bad translation of the Bible because the same teaching is also found in two other places in the Bible, Mark 12:25, and Luke 20:35.

To conclude our discussion of plural wives, when polygamy is mentioned in the Old Testament it is often to point out the problems it caused. The New Testament allows only one wife to church leaders:

> "A bishop then must be blameless, the husband of one wife, vigilant, sober, of good behaviour, given to hospitality, apt to teach" (1 Timothy 3:2).

> "Let the deacons be the husbands of one wife, ruling their children and their own houses well" (1 Timothy 3:12).

The Book of Mormon, which was called "the fulness of my everlasting Gospel" (Doctrine and Covenants 26:5) prohibits plural marriages completely.[1]

In this it is similar to the New Testament which prohibits plural marriages for church leaders. It is, however, diametrically opposed to the "new and everlasting covenant" which requires plural marriage to avoid damnation.[2]

Are we to believe that the "fulness of my everlasting Gospel" which opposed polygamy was abrogated by the "everlasting covenant" which introduced multiple wives to the Church of Jesus Christ of Latter-day Saints? The everlasting covenant only lasted forty seven years before the United States government, and Wilford Woodruff, President of the Church of Jesus Christ of Latter-day Saints, brought it to an end. If either the everlasting Gospel which says, "One wife!" or the everlasting covenant which says, "many wives!" was not really everlasting, the system is wrong, and you submit yourself to it at the risk of your soul.

---

[1] *Book of Mormon*, Jacob 2-24-27.
[2] *Doctrine and Covenants*, 132:4, 6.

3

The Book of Mormon and Church Doctrine

Mormons accept the Bible as sacred Scripture and believe it to be true insofar as it is translated correctly, but their teaching also states:

> "Almost all of the doctrines of the gospel are taught in *The Book of Mormon* with much greater clarity and perfection than those same doctrines are revealed in the Bible."[1]

They elevate *The Book of Mormon* to the place of highest honor among the books which they accept as scripture. They read it, and often think that their religion is based on it, but, other than accepting its historical background, *The Book of Mormon* has hardly been taken into consideration in determining the main distinctive of Mormonism.

This is a serious charge. Let's see if I can back it up.

---

[1]MMD, p. 99.

Many Gods

The Mormon teaching is that there are many gods, not just one. In contrast to both the Bible and *The Book of Mormon*, today's Mormon doctrine teaches that the Father, Son, and Holy Ghost are three Gods rather than one God in three persons. Joseph Smith said later:

"I have always declared God to be a distinct personage, Jesus Christ a separate and distinct personage from God the Father, and the Holy Ghost was a distinct personage and a Spirit: and these three constitute three distinct personages and three Gods."[1] McConkie writes:

> "...and yet they are three separate and distinct entities. Each occupies space and is and can be in but one place at one time, yet each has power and influence that is everywhere present."[2]

Belief in three Gods stands in stark contrast to the Bible: "...I am the LORD, and there is none else" (Isaiah 45:6). Jesus said: "I and my Father are one" (John 10:30).

The Mormon belief in three gods is also completely contrary to the teaching of *The Book of Mormon*:

"...I say unto you, that the Father and the Son, and the Holy Ghost are One; and I am in the Father, and the Father in me, and the Father and I are one."[3]

---

[1]Joseph Fielding Smith, *Teachings of the Prophet Joseph Smith*, 1963, cited by Cowan, *Mormon Claims Answered*, p. 1.
[2]MMD, p. 319.
[3]*Book of Mormon*, 3 Nephi 11:27. See also 2 Nephi 31:21, 1 Nephi 13:41; Mormon 7:7, Alma 11:44.

The Bible and *The Book of Mormon* are in agreement in this point. Both teach one God and not three. The earlier part of *Doctrine and Covenants* is also in agreement. "Which Father, Son, and Holy Ghost are one God, infinite and eternal, without end. Amen."[1]

Mormon doctrine also recognizes a Mother God. "This doctrine that there is a Mother in Heaven was affirmed in plainness by the First Presidency of the church…" and teaches that our spirits were born from the Father God and the Mother God.[2]

That, however, is just the beginning of the Mormon gods. Mormons are taught that those who are married in the temple and obey faithfully to the end will become gods themselves and populate other worlds with their spirit children:

"Mortal persons who overcome all things and gain an ultimate exaltation will live eternally in the family unit and have spirit children, thus becoming Eternal Fathers and Eternal Mothers."[3] They believe that these spirit children will later be born into physical bodies.

Are there really many gods? As we have just seen, the Bible, *The Book of Mormon*, and the early part of *Doctrine and Covenants* all teach that there is only one God. Contradicting all of this is section 132 of *Doctrine and Covenants,* which was written later when Smith wanted to teach Mormons to marry multiple wives. Here he added that in the next life those who followed this new covenant

---

[1]*Doctrine and Covenants* 20:28.
[2]MMD, p. 516.
[3]MMD, p. 517.

would become gods: "Then shall they be gods, because they have all power, and the angels are subject unto them."[1]

What is the most important commandment of all? One day a man asked Jesus:

> "Which is the first commandment of all? And Jesus answered him, The first of all the commandments is, Hear, O Israel; The Lord our God is one Lord: And thou shalt love the Lord thy God with all thy heart, and with all thy soul, and with all thy mind, and with all thy strength: this is the first commandment" (Mark 12:28-30).

Not only is there only one God, there was none before Him, and there will never be another after Him:

> "I am he: before me there was no God formed, neither shall there be after me" (Isaiah 43:10).

There is a certain attraction to believing we will become gods. Satan used this to get Eve to sin against God's commandment to her and Adam when he said to her in the garden:

> "then your eyes shall be opened, and ye shall be as gods, knowing good and evil" (Genesis 3:5).

Lucifer said, "I will be like the most high" (Isaiah 14:14). Whether or not he had any influence on this doctrine in Mormonism, it seems similar.

---

[1]*Doctrine and Covenants* 132:20.

Baptism for the Dead

Mormons study their genealogies, looking for dead relatives who have not been baptized. They are then baptized for them by proxy, hoping that they will have accepted the gospel in the spirit world. If *The Book of Mormon* is right, this practice is useless:

> "For behold, this life is the time for men to meet God…"[1]

> "For behold, if ye have procrastinated the day of your repentance even until death, behold ye have become subjected to the spirit of the devil, and he doth seal you his; therefore the Spirit of the Lord hath withdrawn from you and hath no place in you, and the devil hath all power over you; and this is the final state of the wicked."[2]

These verses state clearly that when one is alive is the time to meet God, and if he puts it off till death the devil seals him, and that is the final state of the wicked. No hope is given of accepting the gospel after death.

Other Mormon Doctrines Foreign to The Book of Mormon

All of the following are doctrines of the Church of Jesus Christ of Latter-day Saints. However, none of them are found in *The Book of Mormon*. In fact, in some cases,

---

[1]*Book of Mormon*, Alma 34:32.
[2]*Book of Mormon*, Alma 34:35.

The Book of Mormon teaches the opposite:
- God as an exalted man
- A heavenly mother
- The degrees of glory
- "The word of wisdom"
  (prohibition of hot drinks: coffee, etc.)
- The pre-existence of people's spirits
- Eternal progression (the belief that men may become gods.) *The Book of Mormon* says that God does not change.[1] For a man to become God would be quite a change.

This is not intended as a complete list, but added to the doctrines that we have already looked at, they are enough to help you understand that *The Book of Mormon* has very little to do with the Mormon distinctives. It does have the stories about migrations to America which Mormons believe are historically true, but not much more. Other than providing a setting for *The Book of Mormon*, the stories of these migrations have little effect on the distinctive beliefs of the Church of Latter-day Saints today.

---

[1]*Book of Mormon*, Mormon 9:9-11, Moroni 8:18

4

Joseph Smith – Background

Joseph Smith was born on December 23, 1805. The *Encyclopedia Britannica* describes his early years: "He was a literate but unschooled lad from a large family, and his neighbors at Palmyra, N.Y. remembered him as a diviner who dug for buried treasure."[1]

Mormon writers have sometimes denied Smith's involvement in occult practices, but the original documents of a court case in which he was found guilty of using these powers to defraud have been found.[2] The following is from these documents:

> "People of State of New York vs. Joseph Smith. Warrant issued upon oath of Peter G. Bridgman, who informed that one Joseph Smith of Bainbridge was a disorderly person and an impostor. Prisoner brought into court March 20

---

[1] *Encyclopedia Britannica* CD 98, Joseph Smith.
[2] Copies available from Utah Lighthouse ministry (www.utlm.org).

(1826). Prisoner examined. Says that he came from town of Palmyra, and had been at the house of Josiah Stowell in Bainbridge most of time since; had small part of time been employed in looking for mines, but the major part had been employed by said Stowell on his farm, and going to school; that he had a certain stone, which he had occasionally looked at to determine where hidden treasures in the bowels of the earth were; that he professed to tell in this manner where gold-mines were a distance under ground, and had looked for Mr. Stowell several times, and informed him where he could find those treasures, and Mr. Stowell had been engaged in digging for them; that at Palmyra he pretended to tell, by looking at this stone, where coined money was buried in Pennsylvania, and while at Palmyra he had frequently ascertained in that way where lost property was, of various kinds; that he has occasionally been in the habit of looking through this stone to find lost property for three years, but of late had pretty much given it up on account its injuring his health, especially his eyes — made them sore; that he did not solicit business of this kind, and had always rather declined having anything to do with this business... And thereupon the Court finds the defendant guilty."[1]

---

[1]www.utlm.org/newsletters/no95.htm

Bills for the services of the Justice of the Peace Albert Neely, who tried the case, and the police officer who brought Smith in have also been found.[1]

"BYU historian Marvin S. Hill has...observed: 'Now, most historians, Mormon or not, who work with the sources, accept as fact Joseph Smith's career as village magician.'"[2]

Smith as a Translator

If Joseph Smith was engaged in witchcraft or other occult practices even before translating *The Book of Mormon*, did these practices have a part in his translation? Joseph tells us that when he started to translate the gold plates of *The Book of Mormon*, he was instructed to use two white stones mounted in silver bows for translating. He called them the Urim and Thummim. Witnesses state, however, that most of his translation was done in a different way, looking into the stone which he had used to search for gold.

I have selected a few of the most important quotes from the witnesses, and other original sources, accompanied by a few comments by the website authors. I have left their references in the text. Statements of other witnesses can be found on the website cited at the end of these quotes:

---

[1] www.utlm.org/newsletters/no95.htm. Also see copies in Walter Martin's, *The Maze of Mormonism*, 1978, p. 37.
[2] *Early Mormonism and the Magic World View*, 2nd edition, 1998, p.59.

"Although Joseph Smith was supposed to have the Urim and Thummim, the evidence shows that he preferred to use the seer stone found in a well to translate *The Book of Mormon*. The Mormon historian B. H. Roberts acknowledged the use of one of Joseph Smith's seer stones. He made the following statement in *History of the Church*, Vol. 1, page 129: 'The Seer Stone referred to here was a chocolate-colored, somewhat egg-shaped stone which the Prophet found while digging a well in the company of his brother Hyrum, for a Mr. Clark Chase, near Palmyra, N.Y. It possessed the qualities of Urim and Thummim, since by means of it — as described above — as well as by means of the Interpreters found with the Nephite record, Joseph was able to translate the characters engraven on the plates.'"

"David Whitmer, one of the three witnesses to *The Book of Mormon*, described how Joseph Smith placed the 'seer stone' into a hat to translate *The Book of Mormon*:

'I will now give you a description of the manner in which *The Book of Mormon* was translated. Joseph would put the seer stone into a hat, and put his face in the hat, drawing it closely around his face to exclude the light. A piece of something resembling parchment would appear, and on that appeared the writing.' (*An Address to All Believers in Christ*, by David Whitmer, 1887, p. 12)

"In a letter written March 27, 1876, Emma Smith acknowledged that the entire *Book of Mormon* that we have today was translated by the use of the seer stone.

James E. Lancaster wrote: 'How can the testimonies of Emma Smith and David Whitmer, describing the translation of *The Book of Mormon* with a seer stone, be reconciled with the traditional account of the church that *The Book of Mormon* was translated by the "interpreters" found in the stone box with the plates? It is the extreme good fortune of the church that we have testimony by Sister Emma Smith Bidamon (Joseph's wife Emma had remarried after his death) on this important issue... a woman... wrote to Emma Bidamon, requesting information as to the translation of *The Book of Mormon*. Emma Bidamon replied... March 27, 1876. Sister Bidamon's letter states in part: 'Now the first that my husband translated, was translated by the use of the Urim and Thummim, and that was the part that Martin Harris lost, after that he used a small stone, not exactly black, but was rather a dark color...'

"Sister Bidamon's letter indicated that at first

The Book of Mormon was translated by the Urim and Thummim. She refers to the instrument found with the plates. However, this first method was used only for the portion written on the 116 pages of foolscap, which Martin Harris later lost. After that time the translation was done with the seer stone. (Saints' Herald, Nov. 15, 1962, page 15; Emma's letter is also reproduced in Early Mormon Documents, Vol. 1, p. 532)"[1]

Smith's Later Years

After finishing *The Book of Mormon* and accumulating followers, Joseph led these early Mormons across the country, settling in one place after another. There was a great deal of violence both from others who lived in the places the Mormons attempted to settle and from the Mormons. Houses were burned and people killed on both sides. In the process Smith built up an army which eventually numbered around 3,000.

Smith wrote that God had given the neighborhood around the Mormon settlement to the Mormons. This, document got into non-Mormon hands causing them to fear that the Mormons would be taking over their lands.

"Antagonism toward the Mormon Prophet was further incited when it was correctly rumored that he had been ordained 'King over the

---

[1]www.utlm.org/newsletters/no95.htm

Immediate House of Israel' by the Council of Fifty. This action was wrongly interpreted by non-Mormons to mean that he was going to attempt to overthrow the United States government by force... his kingly ordination only incensed the populace, and his untimely death became even more inevitable."[1]

In 1844 Joseph Smith became a candidate for president of the United States, but was killed before the election. Marvin Cowan gives a very clear summary of this final chapter in the life of Joseph Smith:

"At the time of his death, Smith was living in Nauvoo Illinois, the second largest city in the state... Nauvoo was a Mormon town and Smith dominated its government as well as its religion. In Nauvoo, Smith began to privately teach Mormon leaders the doctrine of polygamy. When some Mormons heard what their leaders were doing, they vigorously opposed it. But, they did not get much attention until June 7, 1844 when they published the first and only edition of the Nauvoo Expositor newspaper. In it, they exposed Smith's lifestyle and that made him angry. He, along with the Nauvoo City council, declared that the Nauvoo Expositor was a nuisance and had the marshal of the city destroy the press (*History of the*

---

[1]Brigham Young University Studies, Winter 1968, pp. 212-213 cited by: www.utlm.org/onlinebooks/changech17.htm

Church, Vol. 6, pp. 448-454). Those who opposed Smith filed a complaint with the courts in Hancock County, Illinois, saying that Smith had infringed on the freedom of the press. Smith was arrested for riot, but appealed for a writ of Habeas Corpus. He was tried in Nauvoo where he was quickly released. That upset the opposition, who claimed Smith had manipulated the law. The opposition grew until Smith was afraid Nauvoo would be attacked, so he declared martial law. Illinois had granted Nauvoo governmental power like a city-state. They had their own army, the Nauvoo Legion, and Smith was Lieutanant-General of that army. The opposition saw the declaration of martial law as an act of treason against the state of Illinois, so Smith was again arrested and taken to Carthage, Illinois, where he could not influence the court like he did in Nauvoo. It was while Smith was in jail at Carthage that he was killed by a mob."[1]

The Proof of a Prophet

"Beloved, believe not every spirit, but try the spirits whether they are of God: because many false prophets are gone out into the world" (1 John 4:1).

God tells us here that demonic spirits and the prophets who are led by them in their proclamations are out there

---

[1]Cowan, *Mormon Claims Answered*, 1997 edition, p. 10.

trying to deceive. God commands us not to be gullible and just blindly accept spirits which claim to be from Him and people who claim to be His prophets. We should obey God, and check them out. How can we find out if a prophet speaks the word of God or not?

> "But the prophet, which shall presume to speak a word in my name, which I have not commanded him to speak, **or that shall speak in the name of other gods**, even that prophet shall die. And if thou say in thine heart, How shall we know the word which the LORD hath not spoken? When a prophet speaketh in the name of the LORD, **if the thing follow not, nor come to pass**, that is the thing which the LORD hath not spoken, but the prophet hath spoken it presumptuously: **thou shalt not be afraid of him** (Deuteronomy 18:20-22).

Two parts of this passage are important to our discussion:

• The Bible (and *The Book of Mormon*) state clearly that there is only one God. Joseph Smith and the Mormon leadership went on to introduce other gods. This is very severely prohibited in the first part of the passage: "…or that shall speak in the name of other gods, even that prophet shall die."

• If a prophet announces something that does not come to pass, it is not of God, we are not to be afraid of him. In fact, under the Old Testament, he was to be put to death.

Is there any way we can tell if Joseph Smith only gave

true prophecies which came to pass? He wrote out several of his prophecies in *Doctrine and Covenants*. The time limits which he set have now passed, and the prophecies are in a book that you can easily examine yourself. Here is a prophecy that Smith gave in 1832:

> "Which city shall be built, beginning at the temple lot, which is appointed by the finger of the Lord, in the western boundaries of the State of Missouri, and dedicated by the hand of Joseph Smith... Verily this is the word of the Lord, that the city New Jerusalem shall be built by the gathering of the saints, beginning at this place, even the place of the temple, which temple shall be reared in this generation. For verily *this generation shall not all pass away until an house shall be built unto the Lord...*"[1]

This seems to be a prophecy that the Mormons would build a city and a temple in Western Missouri before Joseph Smith's generation died. Have I understood it correctly? In 1870, while many in that generation were still alive, the Apostle Orson Pratt quoted this passage and said:

"God promised in the year 1832 that we should, before the generation then living had passed away, return and build up the temple of the Most High where we formerly laid the corner stone."[2] (See similar quotes from others of

---

[1]*Doctrine and Covenants*, 84:3-4.
[2]*Journal of Discourses*, Vol. 13, p. 362, cited in Cowan, *Mormon Claims Answered*, p. 58.

that generation: vol. 5, p. 134; Vol. 6, p. 956; Vol. 9, p. 71; Vol. 10, p. 344; Vol. 14; p. 275; Vol. 17; p. 111, cited in Tanner, *Mormonism–Shadow or Reality?* p. 189). Pratt, and the other Mormons of the time understood it just like I did.

All have now died. That generation of Mormons did not build the city and the temple in Missouri. The thing called for in this prophecy did not come to pass. Joseph Smith did not pass the test of a true prophet.

Some have tried to counter this with another prophecy by Smith given in the same year, 1832, about the Civil War. Read it in *Doctrine and Covenants* 87. This prophecy was accurate only in stating "the Southern States shall be divided against the Northern States" and in the place where the war would start. Even in this it was right for the wrong reason. The war was generally expected to start right then in 1832 when South Carolina opposed a new tax law. It did not, but in 1861, it started in the same place where people had expected it to start thirty years earlier. Those who use this prophecy to defend Smith as a prophet have to ignore other details of this prophecy which did not come true. Here are a few of them:

• "…slaves shall rise up against their masters who shall be marshaled and disciplined for war" (87:4).

• Great Britain would step in to help the South, thus starting a world war, "and then war shall be poured out upon all nations" (87:3).

• "Plague" (87:6).

• Most important of all, "**a full end of all nations**" (87:6). All nations quite obviously did not come to an end.

Taken as a whole, this prophecy, which is used to brush the false prophecies under the rug, is another false prophecy.

In another of Smith's prophecies given in 1832, the bishop Newel K. Whitney was to warn the cities of New York, Albany, and Boston of judgment if they rejected his gospel:

> "Nevertheless, let the bishop go unto the city of New York, also to the city of Albany, and also to the city of Boston, and warn the people of those cities with the sound of the gospel, with a loud voice, of the desolation and utter abolishment which await them if they do reject these things. For if they do reject these things, the hour of their judgment is nigh, and their house shall be left unto them desolate."[1]

Many years have passed. All those people died much as had the generations before them and those after. Joseph's prophecy missed the mark.

There are many more. Check out *Doctrine and Covenants* 97:19, 111:2-4, Patton was dead before the date set; 124:56-60, a house where Smith's family would live forever and ever. They never lived there. See Marvin Cowan, *Mormon Claims Answered*, pp. 58-66 for details on these and many more unfulfilled prophecies.

Smith made many statements, about salvation and life after death which you can not check out till after you die, and not too many things that you can. That makes the

---

[1]*Doctrine and Covenants*, 84:114-115.

prophecies in which he gave specified time limits very important. Had his statements been accurate, that fact would inspire our confidence in his more important teachings which we can not check out. The ones we can check were wrong. God commands us not to fear a prophet whose prophecies don't pan out. Obey God in this. Why would you want to bet your life that he is right in things you can't check out when he is wrong in things you can check?

A later president of the Church of Jesus Christ of Latter-day Saints, Joseph Fielding Smith, said:

> "Mormonism must stand or fall on the story of Joseph Smith. He was either a Prophet of God, divinely called, properly appointed and commissioned, or he was one of the biggest frauds this world has ever seen. There is no middle ground. If Joseph was a deceiver who willfully attempted to mislead people, then he should be exposed. His claims should be refuted, and his doctrines shown to be false…"[1]

We have examined the evidence:

• In his youth, Joseph Smith was arrested and convicted for using occult practices to defraud.

• Smith claimed to have translated what he called The Book of Abraham from Egyptian manuscripts, though he knew nothing of Egyptian, and his "translation" had nothing to do with the manuscript he claimed to have translated.

---

[1]*Doctrines of Salvation*, 1:188-89, cited in *The Berean Call*, March 2001, p. 8.

• Some of his prophecies clearly did not come to pass.

• From 1890 on, Mormon leaders have asked Mormons not to fulfill a covenant which Smith revealed. He had proclaimed that it was "a new and everlasting covenant; and if ye abide not that covenant, then are ye damned; for no one can reject this covenant and be permitted to enter into my glory."[1] This "new and everlasting covenant" required men to have more than one wife if they were to receive full salvation. Since the present Mormon leaders do not agree with what Joseph Smith wrote about your salvation, how can you be saved?

The Next Step

Chick Publications has a great little tract which tells the story of a court jester, a professional fool, who could always make the king laugh with the crazy things he did and said. One day the king gave the jester a golden scepter, and told him, "My friend, when you find a bigger fool than yourself, you must give him this golden wand."

The jester, wand in hand, walked through all the villages of that country talking to the people, looking for the biggest fool.

Meanwhile, back at the castle, the king became very sick, and as he realized he was dying, he sent messengers to find the jester and bring him back. When the jester came in, the king greeted him in a sad voice and let him know he was dying by saying, "Hello, my little friend, I

---

[1] *Doctrine and Covenants,* 132:4. See also 132:1, 6, 21, 62.

am going on a long, long journey… from which I shall never return!"

"Have you prepared for that journey, your highness?"

"No, I haven't."

"Then I must present this golden wand to you!"

How about you who are reading, have you prepared for that journey?

Baptism

Perhaps you are saying, "Yes, I am prepared. I have been baptized." After we have accepted Christ, we should certainly be baptized, but the apostle Paul, perhaps the greatest missionary who has ever lived, said, "For Christ sent me not to baptize, but to preach the gospel." "For I determined not to know any thing among you, save Jesus Christ, and him crucified" (1 Corinthians 1:14, 17; 2:2).

Why did Christ send him to preach the Gospel rather than to baptize? Paul was not opposed to baptism. It is obvious from his writings that he wanted those who were saved to be baptized, but Christ wanted him to do that which was most important, and baptism does not save. Christ the Savior is the one who saves. How does He save? It was prophesied of Christ seven hundred years earlier:

> "All we like sheep have gone astray; we have turned every one to his own way; and the LORD hath laid on him the iniquity of us all" (Isaiah 53:6).

In the Old Testament God had set up a sacrificial system in which sheep and cows were offered on the altar to cover the sins of the people until the next sacrifice. It was a temporary system that God put in place until the time was right for Christ to come and offer the final and lasting sacrifice:

> "And every priest standeth daily ministering and offering oftentimes the same sacrifices, which can never take away sins: But this man, after he had offered one sacrifice for sins for ever, sat down on the right hand of God" (Hebrews 10:11-12).

The Old Testament sacrifices all looked forward to Jesus Christ who gave Himself as the final and complete sacrifice for our sins. We can trust Christ the Savior to save us, "Who his own self bare our sins in his own body on the tree" (1 Peter 2:24).

After Christ has saved us we should be baptized, but we should be baptized because Christ has saved us, not because we think baptism will do it.

Good Works

Others think they might be prepared for their long trip because they have done good works, and performed ceremonies. If that is what you are thinking, you can never be sure you have done enough, can you? The Bible says:

> "For as many as are of the works of the law are under the curse: for it is written, Cursed is

every one that continueth not in all things
which are written in the book of the law to do
them. But that no man is justified by the law in
the sight of God, is evident: for, The just shall
live by faith. And the law is not of faith: but,
The man that doeth them shall live in them.
Christ hath redeemed us from the curse of the
law, being made a curse for us: for it is written,
Cursed is every one that hangeth on a tree"
(Galatians 3:10-13).

You have every reason to doubt whether your works
will be judged good enough. This passage says, "Cursed is
every one that continueth not in all things which are
written in the book of the law to do them." It says, "all
things," not that it will be okay if you have done some
good works too, to counterbalance your sins. God knows
every bad thing you have ever done, and he is a just judge.
Sin like yours (and mine) has to be paid for. Christ has
paid for our sin. He offers His righteousness and complete
salvation as a free gift. When we accept Christ and the gift
that He offers, our life changes.

I remember trying to clean up my life when I thought
the way to be saved was to quit sinning and only do good
works. I tried as hard as I could, but I was not only unable
to quit the sins that gave me pleasure, I was too weak to
cut back on the sins that brought me no satisfaction at all,
but only humiliation.

It was after I realized that I couldn't do it myself that I
asked Christ to save me. Then the Holy Spirit began to

guide my life and what a change! I was still capable of falling into sin on occasion, but the direction of my life was changed. When I was serving God I was not sinning. When I did fall into sin I confessed it and got up again. I was baptized very soon; not to be saved, but because I had been saved and wanted to please God.

The greatest help in my Christian life was reading the Bible. I immediately got into the habit of reading it a bit every day. It brought me into communion with God and He impressed things on my heart that He wanted me to learn or do.

If I had not started reading the Bible daily, I would soon have been going in my own way again, and thinking it was God's way. The life He gives to those who have believed in him is everlasting:

> "God so loved the world, that he gave his only begotten Son, that whosoever believeth in him should not perish, but have everlasting life" (John 3:16).

We are "kept by the power of God through faith unto salvation ready to be revealed in the last time" (1 Peter 1:5).

Jesus Christ is an exclusive Savior. He does not add a little bit to our salvation by adding to other things that sort of save. He said, "I am the way, the truth, and the life: no man cometh unto the Father, but by me" (John 14:6). If you are trusting Christ, along with baptism and works and temple ceremonies to save you, you are probably not really trusting that Christ can save you. You are thinking that Christ could not completely save you. You need to shift your faith from all those other things you were trusting, and trust the Savior to save you. Wake up to the fact that you need a Savior because you have sinned. Your works don't save, they condemn.

Trust Jesus Christ to be your Savior and Lord! Confess your sins to Him and accept the gift of eternal life that He offers you. He will save you completely. He will not leave you in some level of damnation if you are not married in the temple.

Trust Him also to direct your life every day. Read the Bible daily and it will tell you everything else you need to know to follow Him. You will be ready both for this life, and for your own long trip.

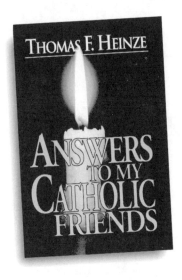

ANSWERS TO MY CATHOLIC FRIENDS

A great little book to give Catholics!

As an evangelical missionary in Italy, Thomas Heinze found that Roman Catholics have certain questions about Protestants, and about the Bible. The ecumenical movement in their own church has made it more important than ever for them to obtain answers to these questions.

Written lovingly to Roman Catholics, this book uses Scriptures to explain major differences between Catholic and Protestant beliefs. So Catholics won't think this is Protestant theology from an "unapproved" Bible, Heinze uses their own New American Bible. Readers quickly see that the Catholic church cannot save, only faith alone in Jesus can.

With a loving, soul-winning message and invitation to trust Christ alone, it's a great book to give Catholics. It's inexpensive too! *62 pages, paperback*

ISBN: 0-937958-52-2
Published by Chick Publications

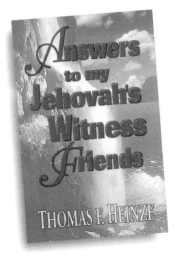

ANSWERS TO MY JEHOVAH'S WITNESS FRIENDS

Answers you need to witness effectively to Jehovah's Witnesses.

When Jehovah's Witnesses come to your door, do you ever wish you could get them off their memorized scripts, and lovingly show them why their religion is wrong? Now you can!

Using many quotes from Watchtower leaders, this small book exposes the errors of this false religion, presenting thought-provoking questions Jehovah's Witnesses can't answer. Don't turn them away from your door saying, "I'm not interested." Learn the facts so you can effectively share the true gospel with them.

This book exposes many unfulfilled Jehovah's Witness prophecies, plus critical facts about: • The 144,000 • Who goes to Heaven? • Eternal punishment • Jesus Christ • The Holy Spirit • The Trinity • The name "Jehovah" • Should we give blood? • Your key to the kingdom • Plus more! *128 pages, paperback*

ISBN: 0-937958-58-1
Published by Chick Publications